The AI Developer's Companion: Mastering Vibe Coding

DEDICATION

To the innovators, the builders, and the dreamers—those who dare to code the future with curiosity, courage, and a touch of AI.

Table of Contents

Introduction

The Dawn of Vibe Coding

Introduction: The Dawn of Vibe Coding

Welcome to the era of Vibe Coding.

When I first started experimenting with AI tools in my development workflow, I didn't realize just how transformative the experience would be. What began as simple autocomplete suggestions quickly evolved into a powerful collaboration between human and machine — a new kind of partnership that has reshaped how I think about problem-solving, code generation, and creativity itself.

"Vibe Coding" is the term I use to describe this emerging practice: working alongside AI tools and Large Language Models (LLMs) to assist, accelerate, and elevate the software development process. It's not just about getting code faster — it's about unlocking new ways of thinking, iterating, and building.

This book is the guide I wish I had when I began that journey.

Drawing from both my experiences and those of other developers who've embraced this shift, I'll walk you through the key principles, tools, and mindset behind effective vibe coding. Whether you're a seasoned engineer looking to integrate AI into your workflow or a curious newcomer eager to learn how to build with an AI assistant at your side, this book will help you get the most out of your coding experience.

We'll cover everything from choosing the right tools, setting up your environment, and planning projects with AI support, to deeper topics like debugging, testing, version control, and even using LLMs for non-coding tasks. Along the way, we'll look at real-world examples, offer practical tips, and most importantly, help you cultivate the skills needed to thrive in this new era of software development.

Vibe coding doesn't replace your creativity or judgment — it enhances it. It helps you move faster, think broader, and build smarter. My hope is that by the end of this book, you won't just understand how to work with AI—you'll enjoy it.

Let's dive in.

CHAPTER 1

Understanding Vibe Coding and the AI Landscape

Chapter 1: Understanding Vibe Coding and the AI Landscape

Vibe coding, at its heart, is about treating AI as an intelligent partner in the development process. It's a form of collaborative programming where the developer provides the direction, context, and refinement, while the AI assists with generating code, suggesting solutions, identifying errors, and handling boilerplate. This is distinct from traditional programming, where the developer is solely responsible for every line of code.

Think of it less like giving commands to a machine and more like working with a highly skilled, albeit sometimes unpredictable, junior developer who has access to an immense knowledge base. Your role is to guide, verify, and integrate their contributions effectively.

The landscape of AI tools for developers is expanding rapidly. These tools can be broadly categorized:

- *Code Editors with Integrated AI:* Tools like Cursor and Windsurf build AI capabilities directly into the coding environment. They can offer real-time code suggestions, generate functions or classes based on comments or prompts, and even refactor code.

- *Standalone LLM Interfaces:* Platforms like ChatGPT, Claude, or specialized coding LLMs provide a chat-based interface where you can ask questions, request code snippets, debug issues, or brainstorm ideas. These are powerful for exploring concepts and generating larger blocks of code or documentation.

- *Specialized AI Tools:* Beyond general-purpose LLMs, there are tools designed for specific tasks, such as AI-powered testing frameworks, documentation generators, or tools for infrastructure management.

Choosing the right tool depends on your needs and experience level. For beginners, integrated environments or user-friendly platforms like Replit with AI features can lower the barrier to entry. More experienced developers might leverage the power of standalone LLMs for complex tasks or integrate AI into their existing preferred editors.

The key takeaway is that vibe coding is not tied to a single tool but is a methodology that can be applied using various AI assistants. The core skill lies in formulating clear requests, understanding the AI's output, and effectively integrating it into your project.

CHAPTER 2

SETTING UP YOUR VIBE CODING ENVIRONMENT

Chapter 2: Setting Up Your Vibe Coding Environment

Getting started with vibe coding requires setting up an environment that facilitates seamless interaction with AI tools while maintaining robust development practices. This involves choosing your primary coding tools and integrating AI capabilities.

Choosing Your Code Editor:

Your code editor is your primary interface with your code. Many modern editors now offer AI integrations, either natively or through plugins. Popular choices include:

- *VS Code*: Highly extensible with a vast marketplace of plugins, including those that integrate with various LLMs.

- *Cursor*: Specifically designed around AI-assisted coding, offering deep integration with models like OpenAI's GPT series.

- *Windsurf*: Another environment built with AI collaboration in mind, providing features to streamline the AI coding workflow.

- Consider features like inline code suggestions, chat interfaces within the editor, the ability to generate code from natural language prompts, and tools for refactoring or explaining code.

Integrating AI Tools:

Once you have your editor, you'll need to integrate your chosen AI tools. This might involve:

- *Installing Editor Plugins*: Many LLMs and AI coding assistants offer plugins for popular editors like VS Code.

- *Using Dedicated AI Coding Environments*: Tools like Cursor or Windsurf are built from the ground up for AI interaction.

- *Accessing Standalone LLMs:* Keep a browser window or a dedicated application open for interacting with standalone LLMs like Claude or ChatGPT for tasks that are better suited for a conversational interface.

Essential Development Practices:

While AI can accelerate coding, it doesn't replace fundamental development practices. Your environment should also be set up for:

- *Version Control:* Absolutely crucial. Ensure you have Git installed and are comfortable using it. Your AI environment should ideally have good Git integration.

- *Testing Frameworks:* Set up the necessary frameworks for writing and running tests (unit, integration, end-to-end) for your chosen programming language and project type.

- *Debugging Tools:* Familiarize yourself with your editor's debugger and how to use it effectively, as you will still need to debug code generated by AI.

- *Documentation Tools:* Consider tools for generating documentation, as maintaining clear documentation is vital, especially when working with AI-generated code.

A well-configured environment minimizes friction and allows you to focus on the creative aspects of development while leveraging AI for assistance. Experiment with different tools and configurations to find what works best for your workflow.

Planning Your Project with AI Assistance

Chapter 3: Planning Your Project with AI Assistance

Effective planning is the bedrock of any successful software project, and AI can be a powerful ally in this initial phase. Instead of just diving into coding, leverage AI to refine your ideas, structure your project, and create a detailed roadmap.

Starting with a Comprehensive Plan:

Begin by creating a comprehensive plan, ideally in a markdown file. Markdown is a great format for this because it's easy to read and structure, and many AI tools are excellent at processing and generating markdown.

Your plan should outline:

- Project Goals and Objectives: What are you trying to achieve? What problems will your software solve?

- Key Features: List the core functionalities your application will have.

- User Stories: Describe how different users will interact with your application.

- Technical Stack: Specify the programming languages, frameworks, databases, and other technologies you plan to use.

- Architecture Overview: A high-level description of how the different components of your application will interact.

- Milestones and Timeline: Break down the project into smaller, manageable phases with estimated completion dates.

Collaborating with the AI on Planning:

This is where the AI comes in. Share your initial ideas and rough plan with your chosen LLM. Ask it to:

- Refine your goals and objectives: The AI can help you clarify your vision and identify potential ambiguities.

- Suggest additional features or use cases: Based on its training data, the AI might propose functionalities you hadn't considered.

- Help structure your plan: Ask the AI to organize your points into a logical flow or suggest a standard project planning template.

- Brainstorm technical approaches: Discuss different architectural patterns or technology choices with the AI to understand their pros and cons.

- Break down complex features: Ask the AI to help you decompose large features into smaller, more manageable tasks.

Working Section by Section:

Once you have a solid outline, work through your plan section by section with the AI. For example, when planning a specific feature:

- Describe the feature in detail to the AI.

- Ask the AI to suggest the necessary components (e.g., backend API endpoints, frontend UI elements, database schema changes).

- Discuss the interactions between these components.

- Ask the AI to outline the steps required to implement this feature.

This iterative process of planning and refinement with the AI helps ensure that your plan is thorough, well-structured, and considers different perspectives. The markdown file becomes a living document that evolves as you collaborate with the AI.

CHAPTER 4

Choosing the Right AI Tools for Your Experience Level

Chapter 4: Choosing the Right AI Tools for Your Experience Level

The world of AI coding tools is diverse, and the best choice for you depends heavily on your existing coding experience and the type of projects you're working on.

For Beginners:

If you're new to coding, AI tools can be incredibly helpful in getting started and understanding fundamental concepts. Look for tools that offer:

- *User-Friendly Interfaces*: Platforms that simplify the coding environment and provide clear guidance.

- *Integrated Learning Resources:* Tools that offer tutorials, explanations, and interactive exercises.

- *Code Generation with Explanations:* AI that not only generates code but also explains why it works and what each part does.

Recommended tools for beginners:

- *Replit:* An online IDE that allows you to write, run, and host code. It has integrated AI features that can help with code completion, debugging, and explaining concepts.

- *Lovable:* With a focus on simplified coding interfaces and guided AI assistance, tools such as Lovable are well-suited for newcomers.

These platforms often abstract away some of the complexities of setting up a development environment, allowing beginners to focus on learning coding concepts with AI support.

For Developers with Some Experience:

If you have some coding experience, you can leverage more powerful AI tools that integrate deeply into your workflow and assist with more complex tasks. Look for tools that offer:

- *Advanced Code Completion and Suggestion:* AI that understands context and provides highly relevant code suggestions.

- *Code Refactoring and Optimization:* Tools that can analyze your code and suggest improvements.

- *Debugging Assistance:* AI that can help you identify and fix errors more quickly.

- *Integration with Popular Editors:* Tools that work seamlessly with your preferred coding environment.

Recommended tools for experienced developers:

- *Windsurf:* An AI-native coding environment designed for collaborative development with AI.

- *Cursor:* A code editor built around AI, offering deep integration with LLMs for code generation, editing, and understanding.

- *Claude Code:* A specialized version of the Claude LLM tuned for coding tasks, offering strong code generation and explanation capabilities.

These tools allow experienced developers to accelerate their workflow, explore new libraries or frameworks more quickly, and tackle more challenging problems with AI assistance.

Experimentation is Key:

The best way to find the right tools is to experiment. Most AI coding tools offer free trials or tiers. Try out a few different options and see which ones fit best with your coding style, the types of projects you work on, and your overall development workflow. The AI landscape is constantly evolving, so be open to trying new tools as they emerge.

Version Control: Your Safety Net in Vibe Coding

Chapter 5: Version Control: Your Safety Net in Vibe Coding

In the world of vibe coding, where AI can rapidly generate and modify code, robust version control is not just a best practice – it's an absolute necessity. Git, the de facto standard for version control, becomes your indispensable safety net, allowing you to track changes, experiment freely, and quickly revert to working states when the AI takes a wrong turn.

Why Git is Crucial with AI:

AI models are powerful, but they are not infallible. They can introduce bugs, make incorrect assumptions, or generate code that doesn't align with your project's architecture or coding standards. Without proper version control, recovering from these issues can be time-consuming and frustrating.

Git allows you to:

- Track Every Change: Every modification made by you or the AI is recorded, giving you a complete history of your project.

- Experiment Safely: Create new branches to experiment with AI-generated code without affecting your main codebase.

- Revert to Previous States: If AI-generated code breaks something, you can easily revert to a previous working commit.

- Identify When Things Broke: By comparing different commits, you can pinpoint exactly when and where an issue was introduced.

- Collaborate Effectively: Even if you're working solo, treating AI as a collaborator means managing its contributions alongside your own — for example, by using commit messages that clearly label AI-generated changes or maintaining separate branches for AI-assisted code.

Using Git Religiously:

Emphasis should be on using Git "religiously." This means:

• Frequent Commits: Commit your code often, with clear and descriptive commit messages. This creates granular checkpoints you can easily return to.

• Branching: Use branches for developing new features or experimenting with AI-generated code. This isolates changes and prevents them from destabilizing your main branch.

• Pull Requests (Even for Solo Projects): If you're working on a team, use pull requests to review AI-generated code before merging it into the main branch. Even for solo projects, creating pull requests from your feature branches can be a good practice for reviewing your own work.

• Understanding Git Commands: While GUI tools exist, having a solid understanding of core Git commands (e.g., add, commit, branch, checkout, merge, log, reset) will give you more control and flexibility.

Integrating Git with Your AI Workflow:

Many AI coding tools have built-in Git integration. Leverage these features to:

• Stage and Commit Changes Directly: Commit AI-generated code directly from your editor.

• View Git History: See the history of changes within your AI coding environment.

• Manage Branches: Create, switch, and merge branches without leaving your editor.

Treating Git as an integral part of your vibe coding workflow will save you significant time and headaches in the long run. It empowers you to leverage the speed of AI while maintaining control and stability over your project.

Chapter 6:
Testing: Validating AI-Generated Code

Chapter 6: Testing: Validating AI-Generated Code

While AI can write code quickly, it doesn't inherently understand the nuances of your project's requirements or the potential edge cases. This is where testing becomes paramount. Writing tests is essential for validating the correctness, reliability, and performance of AI-generated code and ensuring it integrates seamlessly with your existing codebase.

The Importance of Testing in Vibe Coding:

- Verifying Correctness: Tests confirm that the AI-generated code actually does what it's supposed to do according to your specifications.

- Catching Regressions: As you and the AI make changes, tests help ensure that new code doesn't break existing functionality.

- Ensuring Integration: Integration tests specifically verify that different components, including those generated by AI, work together correctly.

- Building Confidence: A comprehensive test suite gives you confidence in deploying your application, knowing that key functionalities are working as expected.

- Identifying Unnecessary Changes: Tests can catch unnecessary changes made by LLMs that might introduce subtle bugs or inefficiencies.

Writing High-Level Integration Tests:

It is highly recommended to write "high-level integration tests." These tests focus on verifying the interaction between different parts of your application and ensuring that end-to-end workflows function correctly.

For example, for a web application, an integration test might simulate a user:

I. Logging in.

II. Navigating to a specific page.
III. Interacting with a form.
IV. Submitting the form.
V. Verifying that the data was processed correctly and the expected result is displayed.

These tests are valuable because they mimic real-world usage and can uncover issues that might be missed by isolated unit tests.

Integrating Testing into Your Workflow:

- Write Tests Before or Alongside Code: Adopt a test-driven development (TDD) approach or write tests concurrently with generating code using AI.

- Automate Your Tests: Set up a testing framework that allows you to run your tests automatically, either manually or as part of a continuous integration (CI) pipeline.

- Use AI to Help Write Tests: You can even ask the AI to help you write tests based on your code or requirements. However, always review and verify the AI-generated tests.

- Run Tests Frequently: Run your test suite regularly, especially after incorporating significant amounts of AI-generated code.

Testing is your primary defense against the potential inaccuracies of AI. By investing time in writing and maintaining a robust test suite, you can confidently leverage the speed of AI code generation while ensuring the quality and stability of your application.

Chapter 7

Beyond Coding: Leveraging LLMs for Non-Coding Tasks

Chapter 7: Beyond Coding: Leveraging LLMs for Non-Coding Tasks

The power of Large Language Models extends far beyond generating code. In the context of software development, LLMs can be invaluable assistants for a wide range of non-coding tasks, streamlining your workflow and freeing up your time for more complex challenges.

Examples of Non-Coding Tasks for LLMs:

- *Configuration Management:* Ask the LLM to help you configure servers, set up deployment pipelines, or write configuration files for various tools and services (e.g., Nginx, Docker, Kubernetes). Provide the AI with the relevant documentation or context, and it can generate the necessary configuration code.

- *Setting Up Hosting and Infrastructure:* LLMs can assist with understanding and configuring cloud hosting services (e.g., AWS, Google Cloud, Azure). Ask for guidance on setting up virtual machines, databases, networking, or serverless functions.

- *Writing Documentation:* LLMs are excellent at generating human-readable text. Use them to:

  - ❖ Write API documentation based on your code.

  - ❖ Create user manuals or tutorials.

  - ❖ Generate README files for your projects.

  - ❖ Explain complex technical concepts.

- *Generating Mock Data:* Need realistic-looking data for testing or development? LLMs can generate structured data in various formats (e.g., JSON, CSV) based on your descriptions.

- *Creating Images and Assets:* While not directly coding, development often involves creating or manipulating assets. Some LLMs or integrated tools can generate images based on text prompts or assist with basic image manipulation tasks like resizing or formatting.

- *Research and Information Gathering:* Use LLMs to quickly find information about libraries, frameworks, APIs, or best practices. While you should always verify the information, LLMs can provide a good starting point for your research.

- *Writing Emails and Communication:* Draft emails to colleagues, clients, or open-source communities with the help of an LLM.

- *Learning New Technologies:* Ask the LLM to explain new concepts, libraries, or frameworks to you. Treat it as a personalized tutor.

Tips for Using LLMs for Non-Coding Tasks:

- *Provide Context:* The more context you give the LLM, the better its output will be. Explain the task clearly, provide relevant details, and specify the desired format.

- *Be Specific:* Instead of asking for "server configuration," ask for "Nginx configuration to serve a static website from this directory."

- *Iterate and Refine:* The first response from the LLM might not be perfect. Provide feedback and ask for revisions until you get the desired output.

- *Verify the Output:* Always double-check the information or configurations provided by the LLM, especially for critical tasks like server setup.

By leveraging LLMs for these non-coding tasks, you can significantly reduce the time spent on administrative or repetitive work, allowing you to focus your energy on the core development challenges.

Chapter 8
Debugging with AI Assistance

Chapter 8: Debugging with AI Assistance

Debugging is an inherent part of the software development process, and AI can be a powerful ally in identifying and fixing errors. LLMs can help you understand error messages, suggest potential causes, and even propose code fixes.

Leveraging AI for Bug Fixes:

- Copy and Paste Error Messages: One of the most effective ways to use AI for debugging is to copy and paste the exact error message you're encountering directly into the LLM. LLMs are trained on vast amounts of code and error logs and can often recognize common error patterns and suggest solutions.

- Explain the Context: Don't just provide the error message. Explain what you were trying to do, what code led to the error, and what you expected to happen. This context helps the AI understand the problem better.

- Ask for Potential Causes: Before jumping to code fixes, ask the AI to list potential causes for the error. This can help you narrow down the possibilities and understand the root of the problem.

- Request Code Fixes: Once you have a better understanding of the potential causes, ask the AI to suggest code modifications to fix the error.

Strategies for Complex Bugs:

For more complex or elusive bugs, a more systematic approach with AI is needed:

- Describe the Bug in Detail: Explain the symptoms of the bug, when it occurs, and what you've already tried to fix it.

- Provide Relevant Code Snippets: Share the code sections that you suspect are related to the bug.

- Ask the AI to Trace the Execution: Describe the expected flow of execution and ask the AI to identify where the code might deviate from that path.

- Discuss Different Debugging Strategies: Ask the AI for suggestions on how to approach debugging the specific type of bug you're facing.

- Reset After Failed Attempts: If an AI-suggested fix doesn't work, revert to the previous working state using version control and try a different approach or ask the AI for alternative solutions. Avoid piling new code on top of a broken state.

Important Considerations:

- Verify AI-Suggested Fixes: Always review and test any code fixes suggested by the AI before implementing them. The AI might not fully understand the intricacies of your specific codebase.

- Don't Blindly Trust the AI: Use the AI's suggestions as a starting point for your own investigation and debugging process.

- Learn from the Process: Pay attention to the AI's explanations and suggestions. This can help you learn more about common error patterns and debugging techniques.

Debugging with AI is a collaborative process. By effectively communicating the problem and providing context, you can leverage the AI's knowledge to significantly speed up the debugging process and resolve issues more efficiently.

Chapter 9
Providing Clear
Instructions to the LLM

Chapter 9: Providing Clear Instructions to the LLM

The quality of the AI's output is directly proportional to the clarity and specificity of your instructions. When vibe coding, treating the LLM as a collaborator requires you to be an effective communicator, providing the AI with the necessary context and guidance to generate the desired code or information.

Key Principles for Giving Instructions:

- *Be Explicit*: Clearly state what you want the AI to do. Avoid ambiguity. Instead of "write some code," say "write a Python function that takes a list of numbers and returns the sum of the even numbers."

- *Provide Context*: Give the AI relevant information about your project, the programming language you're using, the libraries you have available, and the purpose of the code you're requesting.

- *Specify the Desired Output Format*: If you need the code in a specific format (e.g., a function, a class, a complete script), mention it in your instructions. If you need documentation in markdown or a configuration file in YAML, specify that.

- *Break Down Complex Tasks*: For large or complex requests, break them down into smaller, more manageable steps. Ask the AI to complete one step at a time.

- *Use Examples*: Provide examples of the input and expected output for the code you want the AI to generate. This helps the AI understand your requirements more precisely.

- *Define Constraints and Requirements*: Specify any constraints or requirements the code must adhere to, such as performance considerations, memory usage limits, or specific design patterns.

- *Iterate and Refine*: Don't expect the AI to get it perfect on the first try. Review its output and provide feedback to refine the results.

Explain what's wrong and what you'd like to change.

Using Instruction Files:

For larger projects or recurring tasks, consider using "instruction files". These files can contain detailed prompts, context, and requirements that you can easily share with the AI. This ensures consistency in your requests and saves you from having to re-type the same instructions repeatedly.

An instruction file might include:

- A description of the project and its goals.

- Coding style guidelines.

- Information about the technical stack.

- Specific instructions for generating different types of code or documentation.

You can then reference this instruction file when interacting with the AI, saying something like, "Based on the instructions in project_guidelines.md, generate a function to..."

Effective communication with the LLM is a skill that improves with practice. By focusing on clarity, context, and specificity in your instructions, you can significantly enhance the quality and relevance of the AI's output, making your vibe coding experience more productive.

Chapter 10

Documentation:

Keeping Your AI-Assisted Project Clear

Chapter 10: Documentation: Keeping Your AI-Assisted Project Clear

In any software project, clear and accurate documentation is essential for maintainability, collaboration, and understanding the codebase. When working with AI-generated code, documentation becomes even more critical. Since AI can produce code rapidly, it's vital to ensure that you and others can understand why the code was written in a certain way and how it fits into the overall project.

Why Documentation is Crucial with AI:

- Understanding AI-Generated Code: Even with clear prompts, AI-generated code might not always be immediately obvious in its intent or implementation. Documentation helps explain the purpose and logic behind the code.

- Facilitating Collaboration: If you're working in a team, documentation allows other developers to understand the code you've generated with AI and contribute effectively.

- Maintaining the Project: Good documentation makes it easier to maintain and update the codebase in the future, even if the original developer (or AI) is no longer involved.

- Onboarding New Developers: Clear documentation significantly speeds up the process of bringing new team members up to speed on the project.

- Reducing Reliance on the AI for Understanding: While you can ask the AI to explain code, having written documentation provides a stable and readily accessible source of information.

Types of Documentation:

- Code Comments: Add comments within your code to explain complex logic, the purpose of functions or classes, and any non-obvious implementation details.

- API Documentation: Document the inputs, outputs, and behavior of your APIs so that other developers (or your future self) can easily use them.

- Project README: A top-level file that provides an overview of the project, instructions for setting it up and running it, and basic usage examples.

- Architectural Documentation: Describe the high-level design and architecture of your application.

- Decision Logs: Record key technical decisions made during the project, including the reasoning behind them. This is particularly helpful when AI might have suggested multiple approaches.

Using AI to Assist with Documentation:

Just as AI can help write code, it can also assist with generating documentation:

- Generate Code Comments: Ask the AI to add comments to your existing code.

- Draft API Documentation: Provide the AI with your API code or specifications and ask it to generate documentation in a standard format (e.g., OpenAPI, Markdown).

- Create README Files: Give the AI a description of your project and ask it to draft a README file.

- Explain Code Snippets: If you're having trouble understanding a piece of AI-generated code, ask the AI to explain it to you and then use that explanation to write documentation.

Storing Documentation Locally:

It is a good practice to download and store documentation locally for the LLM to access. This is a valuable technique, especially when working with specific libraries, frameworks, or internal APIs. By providing the AI with access to the relevant documentation files, you ensure that its responses are based on accurate and up-to-date information, leading to more correct and relevant code generation and explanations.

Maintaining good documentation is an investment that pays significant dividends throughout the life cycle of your project, especially when working with the dynamic nature of AI-assisted development.

Chapter 11

Learning and Growing with Your AI Companion

Chapter 11: Learning and Growing with Your AI Companion

Vibe coding is not just about getting code generated; it's also a powerful opportunity for learning and professional growth. Your AI companion can serve as a personalized tutor, helping you understand new concepts, explore different approaches, and deepen your understanding of programming.

Using the LLM as a Teacher:

- Explain Code Implementations: If the AI generates a piece of code that you don't fully understand, ask it to explain the implementation line by line or section by section. Ask clarifying questions about specific syntax, functions, or design patterns.

- Understand New Concepts: Encountering a new library, framework, or programming concept? Ask the AI to explain it to you in simple terms, provide examples, and discuss its use cases.

- Explore Different Approaches: If you're unsure about the best way to solve a problem, ask the AI to suggest different approaches and discuss the trade-offs of each.

- Learn Best Practices: Ask the AI about best practices for specific tasks, languages, or frameworks. It can provide insights based on the vast amount of code it has been trained on.

- Refactor and Improve Your Code: Ask the AI to review your existing code and suggest ways to improve its readability, efficiency, or adherence to coding standards. Ask it to explain why its suggestions are improvements.

Beyond Explanations:

Learning with AI goes beyond just getting explanations. It also involves:

- Experimentation: Use the AI to quickly prototype and

experiment with new ideas or technologies without the overhead of setting everything up manually.

- Exposure to Diverse Code: By generating code for various tasks and in different styles, the AI can expose you to a wider range of coding patterns and techniques than you might encounter in your daily work.

- Identifying Knowledge Gaps: As you interact with the AI and ask questions, you'll naturally identify areas where your own knowledge is lacking, guiding your further learning.

Continuous Learning in a Changing Landscape:

The field of AI and its application in software development is evolving at an incredible pace. New models, tools, and techniques are emerging constantly. To stay effective in vibe coding, continuous learning is essential.

- Experiment with New Models: Continuously experiment with new AI models as they become available. Different models have different strengths and weaknesses.

- Stay Updated on AI Research: Follow blogs, research papers, and news related to AI in software development to understand the latest advancements.

- Share Your Experiences: Discuss your experiences with vibe coding with other developers. Share tips, challenges, and discoveries (which is the main purpose of this book).

Treat your AI companion not just as a tool for generating code but as a valuable resource for expanding your knowledge and skills. Embrace the opportunity to learn alongside the AI and grow as a developer in this dynamic new era.

Chapter 12
Handling Complex Functionality with AI

Chapter 12: Handling Complex Functionality with AI

While AI is adept at generating boilerplate and handling common tasks, tackling complex functionality requires a more strategic approach. Simply asking the AI to build an entire complex system is unlikely to yield a perfect result. Instead, focus on breaking down complexity and using AI to assist with specific parts.

Breaking Down Complexity:

The key to handling complex functionality with AI is to decompose it into smaller, more manageable components.

- Define the Complex Feature: Clearly articulate the complex feature you want to implement.

- Break it Down: Identify the individual sub-components or steps required to build the feature.

- Define the Interfaces: Specify how these sub-components will interact with each other.

- Address Each Component Individually: Work on implementing each sub-component, leveraging AI assistance for each part.

Creating a Standalone Reference Implementation:

For particularly complex features, consider creating a "standalone reference implementation." This involves building a simplified, self-contained version of the complex functionality outside of your main project.

Why do this?

- Isolate the Problem: Working in a standalone environment allows you to focus solely on the complex logic without being distracted by the rest of your project.

- Experiment Freely: You can experiment with different approaches and algorithms in the reference implementation without risking your main codebase.

- Provide a Clear Example for the AI: Once you have a working reference implementation, you can provide it to the AI as a clear example of what you want to achieve.

Using the Reference Implementation with the AI:

- Share the Reference Code: Provide the AI with the code for your standalone reference implementation.

- Explain the Goal: Clearly explain that you want to reimplement this functionality within your larger project.

- Specify the Context: Tell the AI where this functionality needs to fit into your existing codebase, including any dependencies or interfaces.

- Request Reimplementation: Ask the AI to generate the code for the complex feature based on the reference implementation and the context of your project.

The AI can then use the reference implementation as a guide, understanding the logic and structure of the complex functionality. This significantly increases the chances of the AI generating correct and relevant code for your main project.

Iterative Development:

Implementing complex features, even with AI assistance, is often an iterative process. Start with a basic implementation and gradually add complexity, testing and refining as you go. Use AI to help with each iteration, generating code for new sub-components or refining existing ones.

By breaking down complexity, using reference implementations, and adopting an iterative approach, you can effectively leverage AI to tackle even the most challenging functionalities in your projects.

Chapter 13

MODULARITY: DESIGNING FOR AI COLLABORATION

Chapter 13: Modularity: Designing for AI Collaboration

Designing your codebase with modularity in mind is crucial when working with AI. A modular architecture, characterized by small, well-defined files and components, makes your project easier for both humans and AI to understand, navigate, and modify.

What is Modularity?

Modularity is a software design principle that emphasizes breaking down a system into smaller, independent, and interchangeable modules. Each module should have a single, well-defined responsibility and a clear interface for interacting with other modules.

Why Modularity is Important for Vibe Coding:

- *Easier for AI to Process*: LLMs have limitations on the amount of code they can process at once. Smaller files and modules are easier for the AI to understand and generate code for.

- *Reduced Risk of Errors*: When the AI works on a small, focused module, there's less chance of it introducing unintended side effects in other parts of the codebase.

- *Improved Code Generation Accuracy*: With a clear understanding of a module's purpose and its interactions with other modules, the AI can generate more accurate and relevant code.

- *Simplified Debugging*: When an issue arises, a modular structure makes it easier to isolate the problem to a specific module, simplifying the debugging process.

- *Enhanced Maintainability*: Modular code is generally easier to maintain and update, as changes to one module are less likely to affect others.

- *Better Collaboration:* Both human developers and AI can work on different modules concurrently without stepping on each other's toes.

Implementing Modularity:

- *Single Responsibility Principle:* Design your functions, classes, and modules to have a single, well-defined responsibility.

- *Clear Interfaces:* Define clear and stable interfaces for how your modules interact with each other.

- *Small File Sizes:* Keep your code files relatively small and focused on a specific task or component.

- *Logical Organization:* Organize your files and directories in a logical structure that reflects the modular design of your application.

- *Avoid Tight Coupling:* Minimize dependencies between modules. Modules should interact through their defined interfaces rather than having direct knowledge of each other's internal implementation details.

Using AI to Promote Modularity:

You can use AI to help you design and implement a modular architecture:

- Ask for Design Suggestions: Describe your project to the AI and ask for suggestions on how to break it down into modules.

- Generate Module Templates: Ask the AI to generate boilerplate code for new modules based on your specifications.

- Refactor Existing Code: If you have a monolithic codebase, use AI to help you refactor it into smaller, more modular components.

- Generate Interface Definitions: Ask the AI to help you define clear interfaces between your modules.

By prioritizing modularity in your project design, you create a codebase that is not only easier for humans to work with but also significantly improves the effectiveness and reliability of your AI coding companion.

Chapter 14
Choosing Your Tech Stack Wisely

Chapter 14: Choosing Your Tech Stack Wisely

The technical stack you choose for your project can have a significant impact on your experience with vibe coding. While AI models are trained on vast amounts of data, they tend to perform better with technologies that are widely used and have extensive documentation available online.

The Impact of Tech Stack on AI Performance:

- Training Data: AI models learn from the data they are trained on. Technologies with a large presence on the internet (code repositories, documentation, forums) provide more training data for the AI, leading to better understanding and code generation.

- Documentation Availability: AI can leverage online documentation to generate more accurate and relevant code. Technologies with comprehensive and easily accessible documentation are more likely to result in better AI assistance.

- Community Support: Popular technologies often have large and active communities. This means more examples, tutorials, and solutions to common problems are available online, which the AI can draw upon.

Well-Established Frameworks:

As mentioned earlier, using well-established frameworks—such as Ruby on Rails, which benefit from abundant training data—is a key consideration in vibe coding. This underscores the advantage of choosing mature technologies when working with AI.

Examples of well-established frameworks and languages with extensive online presence include:

- *Web Development*: React, Angular, Vue.js (Frontend), Node.js, Django, Flask, Ruby on Rails, Spring (Backend)

- *Mobile Development*: Swift (iOS), Kotlin (Android), React Native,

Flutter

- *Data Science:* Python (with libraries like Pandas, NumPy, scikit-learn), R

While AI can work with less common technologies, you might find that the code generated is less accurate, requires more refinement, or that the AI has difficulty understanding specific nuances of the language or framework.

Experimentation and Niche Technologies:

This doesn't mean you should avoid experimenting with new or niche technologies. However, when working with them, be prepared to:

- Provide More Context: You'll need to provide the AI with more specific instructions and potentially relevant code snippets or documentation for less common technologies.

- Verify Output More Carefully: The AI's output might be less reliable, requiring more thorough review and testing.

- Supplement with Manual Coding: You might need to write more code yourself when working with technologies that the AI is less familiar with.

Balancing Innovation and AI Compatibility:

Choosing a tech stack involves balancing the needs of your project, your team's expertise, and the potential benefits of AI assistance. For projects where leveraging AI for rapid development is a high priority, opting for a well-established tech stack can significantly enhance your vibe coding experience. For projects that require cutting-edge or specialized technologies, be prepared to invest more time in guiding and verifying the AI's contributions.

Chapter 15
Additional Tips for Effective Vibe Coding

Chapter 15: Additional Tips for Effective Vibe Coding

Beyond the core principles, several additional tips can help you maximize your effectiveness when vibe coding and make the process smoother and more productive.

Using Screenshots:

It is highly recommended to use screenshots to demonstrate UI bugs or design inspiration. This is a simple yet powerful technique.

- Reporting UI Bugs: If you encounter a visual bug in your application, take a screenshot and share it with the AI. Explain what's wrong and what you expect to see. The visual context can help the AI understand the problem better than a text description alone.

- Communicating Design Ideas: If you have a design in mind or see an element on another website or application that you want to replicate, take a screenshot and share it with the AI. Ask the AI to generate the code to create a similar element or layout.

Using Voice Input:

For faster interaction with LLMs, consider using voice input. Many AI interfaces and operating systems offer speech-to-text capabilities.

- Dictate Prompts: Instead of typing out long prompts, dictate them to the AI. This can be significantly faster, especially when you have a clear idea of what you want to request.

- Explain Code Verbally: Explain code snippets or debugging scenarios verbally to the AI.

While voice input can be convenient, be mindful of potential transcription errors and ensure the AI accurately understands your spoken instructions.

Refactoring Frequently with Implemented Tests:

Refactoring, the process of restructuring existing code without changing its external behavior, is a crucial practice for maintaining code quality. When vibe coding, refactoring frequently is even more important because AI-generated code might not always adhere to your preferred style or architecture.

- **Improve Code Readability:** Use AI to help you refactor code to make it more readable and understandable.

- **Optimize Performance:** Ask the AI to suggest ways to optimize your code for better performance.

- **Align with Design Patterns:** Refactor code to align with established design patterns.

The key is to perform refactoring with implemented tests. Your test suite acts as a safety net, ensuring that your refactoring efforts haven't introduced any regressions or broken existing functionality. Run your tests after every refactoring session to verify that everything is still working correctly.

Experiment Continuously:

The field of AI is rapidly evolving. New models are released, existing models are updated, and new tools and techniques for vibe coding are constantly emerging. To stay at the forefront of this field, it's essential to experiment continuously.

- **Try New AI Models:** Explore different LLMs and see how they perform for different tasks.

- **Experiment with New Tools:** Try out new AI coding environments, plugins, and specialized AI tools.

- **Explore New Techniques:** Experiment with different prompting strategies, ways of structuring your interactions with the AI, and methods for integrating AI into your workflow.

The vibe coding landscape of today might look very different from the landscape a few months or a year from now. By embracing experimentation, you can discover new ways to leverage AI and stay ahead of the curve.

CONCLUSION

EMBRACING THE FUTURE OF SOFTWARE DEVELOPMENT

Conclusion: Embracing the Future of Software Development

Vibe coding represents a significant evolution in the practice of software development. It's a shift from the solitary programmer meticulously crafting every line of code to a collaborative process where human creativity and problem-solving are augmented by the power of Artificial Intelligence.

Throughout this book, we've explored the core principles and practical techniques for effectively leveraging AI in your development workflow. We've discussed the importance of planning, the necessity of robust version control and testing, the value of using AI for non-coding tasks, and the art of communicating effectively with your AI companion. We've also highlighted the significance of documentation, continuous learning, handling complexity, designing for modularity, and choosing your tech stack wisely.

The key takeaway is that vibe coding is not about replacing the developer but about empowering them. By mastering the techniques of vibe coding, you can:

- Accelerate Your Development Speed: Offload repetitive tasks and generate code more quickly.

- Improve Code Quality: Leverage AI's knowledge to write more efficient, readable, and bug-free code.

- Explore New Solutions: Brainstorm ideas and explore different approaches with your AI companion.

- Focus on Higher-Level Challenges: Spend more time on architectural design, complex problem-solving, and creative innovation.

- Continuously Learn and Grow: Use AI as a tool for expanding your knowledge and skills.

The landscape of AI in software development will continue to evolve. New tools will emerge, models will become more capable, and the ways we interact with AI will become more sophisticated. By staying curious, experimenting continuously, and embracing the principles of effective vibe coding, you will be well-equipped to thrive in this exciting future of software development.

The AI Developer's Companion is a journey, not a destination. As you continue to practice and experiment with vibe coding, you will discover new techniques and refine your workflow. Embrace the collaborative nature of working with AI, treat it as a powerful tool to enhance your abilities, and enjoy the process of building amazing software in this new era.

Happy Vibe Coding!